abbreviation

An abbreviation is  a group of words.

- Dr (Doctor), NH (Local Education Authority), Ltd (Limited)

acronym

This is an abbreviation made up of the first letters of a group of words, pronounced as one word.

- NATO (North Atlantic Treaty Organisation) RAM (Random Access Memory)

adjective

An adjective is a word that describes somebody or something.

The adjective may come before or after the noun.

- The **strange**, **little** dog with the **long** tail
- The **red** dress
- The dress was **red**.

adverb

An adverb is a word or phrase which gives more information about a verb, an adjective, another adverb or a whole sentence. An adverb often tells how, when or where something is done. They often end in -ly.

- Please come **here**.
- She speaks **quickly** and **quietly**.

alliteration

This is a group of words that begin with the same sound.

- Several silent slithering snakes

antonym

A word which means the opposite of another word is an antonym.

Many words have more than one antonym.

- hot – cold
- big – small / tiny / little

apostrophe

An apostrophe is a punctuation mark (') that is used to show ownership or to show that a word has been shortened by missing out letters.

- **Sameea's** book, the **doctors'** surgery, the **girl's** coat, the **children's** playground, **I'm** afraid there **aren't** any tea-bags left.

autobiography

A life story written by that person is an autobiography.

- *Long Walk to Freedom*, Nelson Mandela

a

a
b
c
d
e
f
g
h
i
j
k
l
m
n
o
p
q
r
s
t
u
v
w
x
y
z

a

a
b
c
d
e
f
g
h
i
j
k
l
m
n
o
p
q
r
s
t
u
v
w
x
y
z

ballad

A ballad is a poem or song that tells a story.

- Frankie and Johnny were sweethearts

bibliography

A list of books or articles is a bibliography.

biography

A biography is the life story of a person, written by someone else.

- *Posh and Becks*, Andrew Morton

b

b

chronological writing

This is writing that describes events in the order in which they took place.

- many historical accounts, police reports

cliché

A cliché is a word or phrase that has been used so often it loses its impact.

- As sick as a parrot
- At this moment in time
- We'll leave no stone unturned.

comma

A comma is a punctuation mark (,) used to help the reader by separating parts of a sentence.

- I swear I will tell the truth, the whole truth, and nothing but the truth.

connective

Words and phrases which are used to link parts of a text are connectives. They may be used to make two or more simple sentences into one compound sentence. They may also be used to connect sentences or ideas in a paragraph.

- **but, although, while, if, so that**
- I chose red **because** it's my favourite colour.
- He loaded the washing machine **before** he started watching television.

consonant

All the letters of the alphabet except the vowels are consonants.

'Y' can act as either a vowel or a consonant.

- b c d f g h j k l m n p q r s t v w x y z
- 'y' in 'yes', 'you', 'yellow'

consonant cluster or consonant blend

A group of consonants together.

- 'str' in 'street'.

apostrophe – auto-biography

C

a
b
c
d
e
f
g
h
i
j
k
l
m
n
o
p
q
r
s
t
u
v
w
x
y
z

dialogue

This is a written or spoken conversation between two people.

diphthong

A **vowel** with a noticeable sound change within the same **syllable**.

- 'm**u**sic' or 'b**oi**l'

discussion

This is a text type that presents arguments and information from different points of view.

- Arguments for and against a town bypass

d

d

etymology

Etymology is the study of the origin and history of words.

- bi (Latin meaning two): bilingual, bifocals, bicycle
- centum (Latin meaning 100): century, centurion, cent, percentage
- scribere (Latin meaning to write): script, inscription, scribe
- phobos (Greek meaning fear): phobia, agoraphobia
- demos (Greek meaning people): democratic

exclamation mark

This is a punctuation mark (!) used at the end of a sentence to show a strong feeling or emotion like surprise, joy, pain or anger.

- Stop!   Oh!   Fire!

explanation

This is a text type that explains how or why something happens or how it works.

- The life cycle of a butterfly
- How different vehicles work

e

e

e

fiction

A work in which what happens has been invented by the writer.

- Novels, TV dramas, short stories

footnote

Additional information printed at the bottom of the page is a footnote.

- See E

f

a
b
c
d
e
f
g
h
i
j
k
l
m
n
o
p
q
r
s
t
u
v
w
x
y
z

f

a
b
c
d
e
f
g
h
i
j
k
l
m
n
o
p
q
r
s
t
u
v
w
x
y
z

genres

These are different types of writing, each with their own specific characteristics.

- Science-fiction, historical novels, myth, biography, diary

glossary

A glossary is a list of words or terms and their definitions.

- Literacy – reading, writing, speaking and listening

g

g

g

high-frequency words

Words that are used often which have little meaning on their own but contribute to the meaning of a sentence.

- and, the, is, it

homophone

Words which sound the same but have a different meaning are homophones.

- pair / pear   right / write   meet / meat
  which / witch   road / rowed

hyphen

A hyphen is a punctuation mark (-) used to join two words or to divide a word that runs over from one line to the next.

- cross-reference

h

h

idiom, idiomatic language

This is an expression that does not make sense if you take the individual words literally.

- You look a **bit under the weather** today.
- That will **cut no ice** with the manager.
- That name **rings a bell**. I know I have heard it somewhere.

instruction

This is a text type that aims to help the reader complete a task or achieve a goal.

- Recipes
- Instructions on playing a board game
- How to put furniture together

i

a
b
c
d
e
f
g
h
i
j
k
l
m
n
o
p
q
r
s
t
u
v
w
x
y
z

i

a
b
c
d
e
f
g
h
i
j
k
l
m
n
o
p
q
r
s
t
u
v
w
x
y
z

jargon

Specialised language used by particular groups (sometimes to exclude others) is called jargon.

- ESOL learners

j

- a
- b
- c
- d
- e
- f
- g
- h
- i
- **j**
- k
- l
- m
- n
- o
- p
- q
- r
- s
- t
- u
- v
- w
- x
- y
- z

j

j

a
b
c
d
e
f
g
h
i
j
k
l
m
n
o
p
q
r
s
t
u
v
w
x
y
z

k

k

a
b
c
d
e
f
g
h
i
j
k
l
m
n
o
p
q
r
s
t
u
v
w
x
y
z

legend

This is a traditional story about heroic characters.

- King Arthur and the Knights of the Round Table
- Robin Hood

long vowel sounds

Each vowel can make a short sound and a long sound.

- **a**t or **a**te, or **e**gg or m**ee**t

l

I

- a
- b
- c
- d
- e
- f
- g
- h
- i
- j
- k
- l
- m
- n
- o
- p
- q
- r
- s
- t
- u
- v
- w
- x
- y
- z

metalanguage

Language we use to describe how language works is called metalanguage.

- sentence, noun, paragraph

mnemonic

A mnemonic is a catchphrase or way of remembering difficult spellings.

- There's a **rat** in sep**ar**ate.
- One collar two sleeves – ne**css**ary
- Station**e**ry or station**a**ry? There's an e in envelopes.

monologue

This is a text spoken by just one person (unlike a dialogue where there are two people speaking).

morpheme

A morpheme is the smallest unit of meaning. A word can be one morpheme, two morphemes, three morphemes.

- house – one morpheme
- house/s – two morphemes
- house/keep/ing – three morphemes

myth

A myth is an ancient traditional story.

- Romulus and Remus
- Daedalus and Icarus

m

m

a
b
c
d
e
f
g
h
i
j
k
l
m
n
o
p
q
r
s
t
u
v
w
x
y
z

narrative

This is a text that re-tells events, often in chronological order.

non-chronological report

This is a text type that describes the way things are without referring to a time sequence.

- a guidebook

non-fiction

Different texts based on facts are known as non-fiction.

- reference book, report, manual, instructions

noun

A noun is a word that names something or somebody.

A proper noun is a specific name and starts with a capital letter.

- man, shop, town, street
- Jim, Tesco, Leicester, Station Road.

n

a
b
c
d
e
f
g
h
i
j
k
l
m
n
o
p
q
r
s
t
u
v
w
x
y
z

n

n

onomatopoeia

Onomatopoeia means words in which the sound echoes the meaning.

- hiss, crash, cuckoo

onset and rime

The onset is the initial consonant or consonant cluster of a word.

Some words have no onset.

The rime is the part of a syllable which contains the vowel and final consonant(s).

- **cl**ub, **tr**ain, **p**an, **s**un
- 'use' and 'out' have no onset
- t**orn**, f**eel**, th**atch**, spl**ash**

o

O

paragraph

A paragraph is a section of a piece of writing. Each paragraph begins on a new line. It marks a change of focus e.g. time, place, new character speaking.

parable

This is a short story with a moral.

- The story of the Good Samaritan

persuasion

This is a text type that aims to persuade the reader.

- healthy eating leaflet, advertisements

phoneme

The smallest unit of sound in a word is a phoneme. It may be represented by 1, 2, 3 or 4 letters.

- t**o**, sh**oe**, cr**ew**, thr**ough**

phonics

An approach to teaching reading and spelling which focuses on linking phonemes (speech sounds) with graphemes (letters or groups of letters).

prefix

A prefix is a morpheme added to the beginning of a word to change its meaning.

- **un**happy, **dis**approve, **anti**freeze, **mis**understand, **pre**school

pronoun

A pronoun is a word used in place of a noun.

- He, him, mine, it

punctuation

Punctuation marks help the reader to know how to read text with the correct expression.

- Common punctuation marks are full stop, comma, apostrophe, question mark and exclamation mark.

p

a
b
c
d
e
f
g
h
i
j
k
l
m
n
o
p
q
r
s
t
u
v
w
x
y
z

question mark

A punctuation mark (?) which is used at the end of a sentence to show that it is a question, is called a question mark.

It helps the reader to know how to read the text with the correct expression.

- Where do you live?
- You live in Leicester?

q

q

recount

This is a text type that retells events in the order that they took place.

- a newspaper report, a biography.

r

a
b
c
d
e
f
g
h
i
j
k
l
m
n
o
p
q
r
s
t
u
v
w
x
y
z

r

a
b
c
d
e
f
g
h
i
j
k
l
m
n
o
p
q
r
s
t
u
v
w
x
y
z

scan

A reading strategy to find a particular piece of information from a piece of text that doesn't involve reading every word.

sentence

A sentence is a group of words that makes sense by itself.

Sentences start with a capital letter, end with a full stop and contain a verb.

- The dog bit him.
- The entire village was ruined by the hurricane and people had no shelter for many days.
- Would you like coffee or tea?

silent letters

These are letters that make no sound.

- 'si**g**n' 'lis**t**en' or '**w**rap'

short vowel sounds

Each vowel can make a short sound and a long sound.

- at or ate, or egg or meet

skim

This is a way of reading to get a quick first impression of the meaning.

suffix

A morpheme added to the end of a word is the suffix.

- talk**ing**, amuse**ment**, slow**ly**, tree**s**, work**ed**

syllable

A unit of spoken language with one sound that forms the whole or a part of a word.

- The word syllable has three sylables

  syl·la·ble

synopsis

A brief summary of the main points in a book or an article is called a synopsis.

synonym

Synonyms are words which have the same or similar meanings.

- wet / damp   easy / simple
  true / right / correct / accurate / certain

synthetic phonics

Synthetic phonics is an approach to learning to read which starts with letter sounds then puts them together, or synthesises them, to blend together in order to pronounce whole words.

S

S

text types

Text types are different kinds of writing.

- discussion, explanation, instruction, fiction, narrative, non-chronological report, non-fiction, recount, persuasion

thesaurus

A thesaurus is a reference book that lists alternative words with similar meanings.

- fast, swift, quick, rapid, hasty, speedy

t

t

u

verb

A verb is a word or group of words which names an action, a happening, a process or state of being.

- do, go, eat,
- have done, is going, will eat

vowel

There are 5 vowels.

'Y' can act as either a vowel or a consonant.

- a, e, i, o, u
- 'y' in 'happy', 'fly'

V

a
b
c
d
e
f
g
h
i
j
k
l
m
n
o
p
q
r
s
t
u
V
w
x
y
z

v

writing frame

A structured outline to support different kinds of writing is called a writing frame.

- A framework to complete a letter or CV
- Opening phrases for a story to be continued by the writer

w

- a
- b
- c
- d
- e
- f
- g
- h
- i
- j
- k
- l
- m
- n
- o
- p
- q
- r
- s
- t
- u
- v
- **w**
- x
- y
- z

w

- a
- b
- c
- d
- e
- f
- g
- h
- i
- j
- k
- l
- m
- n
- o
- p
- q
- r
- s
- t
- u
- v
- **w**
- x
- y
- z

X

- a
- b
- c
- d
- e
- f
- g
- h
- i
- j
- k
- l
- m
- n
- o
- p
- q
- r
- s
- t
- u
- v
- w
- **x**
- y
- z

y

Z

a
b
c
d
e
f
g
h
i
j
k
l
m
n
o
p
q
r
s
t
u
v
w
x
y
z

a
b
c
d
e
f
g
h
i
j
k
l
m
n
o
p
q
r
s
t
u
v
w
x
y
z